SCOTLAND'S MUSIC

SCOTLAND'S MUSIC

CEDRIC THORPE DAVIE

William Blackwood
Edinburgh

William Blackwood
32 Thistle Street
Edinburgh EH2 1HA

First published 1980
© Cedric Thorpe Davie

ISBN 0 85158 136 6

Printed by William Blackwood & Sons Ltd

Contents

Introduction

What do we mean by 'Scottish music'? At first glance, the question presents no particular difficulty; however, a little thought reveals a good many uncertainties and raises several further questions. By 'Scottish music', do we mean music that has some ascertainable and unique Scottish quality? Or do we mean music originated in Scotland, either anonymously by way of a folk tradition or in the mind of a native Scot? That begs the question, 'What is a native Scot?' and poses additional questions: is music composed by a Scot domiciled in the U.S.A., for example, to be regarded as Scottish? Or, conversely, music composed by a non-Scot living in Scotland? Further uncertainties appear when we consider the assimilation of French and other tunes into the musical tradition of the Church of Scotland, or the floods of pseudo- and imitation Scottish songs that have from time to time during the past three centuries enjoyed huge popularity, of which only a fraction have originated in Scotland. What about arrangements of Scottish songs by eminent Continental composers like Haydn and Beethoven? What about the deliberate interpolation of Scottish tunes into instrumental variations and concertos by composers of high standing in their day, such as Pleyel and J. C. Bach? Is the description 'Scottish' to be applied to importations like *Brigadoon*, which reflect a romanticised Scotland viewed through the rose-tinted spectacles of sentimental Americans?

I will try to answer these and other questions as they arise. I have somewhat arbitrarily divided the material into three parts. The first is concerned with what has come to be known as Scottish National Music; it includes genuine folk music for voices or instruments, as well as a large body of usually more sophisticated material, most of which derives in some way from folk music through the deliberate acts of poets and musicians. The second and shortest part deals with the music of the church in Scotland, both before and after the Reformation, while the third has to do with Scottish 'classical' music, using the word in its popular sense; that is to say, it is a survey of composers, the bulk of whose output is specifically designed as a contribution to the Art of Serious Music.

Of necessity, Part Three is superficial, and those who wish to look more deeply into the matter are recommended to consult the works mentioned in the short select bibliography, to avail themselves of the excellent facilities offered by the Scottish Music Archive, and above all to miss no opportunity of listening to the music itself, live if possible.

I am aware that this broad division is open to criticisms— particularly that I must set myself up as arbiter of what is or is not to be included in the Art of Serious Music; and that there is also a vast body of music near the borderline, about which opinions will differ. Nevertheless, I see no other way of reducing the material to manageable proportions, and I must hope and trust that readers will show sympathetic understanding of this handling of the subject.

It can be argued that the music discussed in Part Three is the *successor* to a simpler, more spontaneous Scottish product, and that a certain naïvety found in much of the older music has given way to more sophisticated attitudes and techniques. Any author who maintained such a view would quickly bring upon himself a shower of brickbats, hurled by enthusiasts claiming that the Scottish folk tradition is not a relic of the past, but a still-living thing, expressive of the soul of the nation. He would, moreover, be ignoring, or at least minimising, the influence of the older music upon the newer—an influence which was for long welcomed and deliberately fostered and exploited by composers of the past century or so. Even if it be admitted that the second half of the twentieth century has seen a diminution of conscious attempts at 'Scottishness' on the part of composers, and a move towards a more international mode of expression, there is no way of proving that this is more than a phase in the evolution of Scottish musical culture. Only the passage of time will settle the matter, and we must be content to allow posterity, with its remarkable capacity for sifting chaff from wheat, to decide to what extent today's native product is specifically Scottish.

The National Music of Scotland

VOCAL MUSIC IN THE LOWLANDS

O sing to me the auld Scots sangs
I' the braid Scottish tongue,
The sangs my father wish'd to hear,
The sangs my mither sung.

This somewhat ungrammatical request was made by the Rev. Dr Bethune in the mid-nineteenth century and set to music by an Irishman named Joseph Leeson in a drawing-room ballad which achieved such popularity that to many it acquired the status of an Auld Scots Sang in its own right. Its clear implication is that the poet's mother had a repertoire of well-known and well-loved traditional melodies ready to produce on intimate family occasions.

A little investigation reveals that the customary term 'Scots Song' covers a huge body of vocal music ranging from marvellous folk ballads of unknown origin and inestimable age to commercial potboilers produced to satisfy a recurrent public demand not only in Scotland, but in the theatres, pleasure gardens and drawing-rooms of London, Dublin and elsewhere. This demand first began in the late seventeenth century, and is clearly discernible at other points in British history; indeed, it is strong at the present time and, artificially stimulated by all the apparatus of modern publicity, has spread to Canada, Australia, the U.S.A. and other parts where there are many descendants of Scots émigrés.

At one end of the scale we have such ancient ballads as the deeply tragic and moving 'The Braes of Yarrow' in its multifarious forms; at the other, a profusion of sentimental songs about heather, misty islands, and the recollections of private soldiers, particularly concerning their grandmothers' rose-covered cottages in the Highlands. Between these extremes lies an infinitely graded mass of material, much of it the result of fitting new words to old tunes, by poets like Allan Ramsay and Robert Burns; the total is further augmented by deliberately composed songs of varying quality, some of which—'Annie Laurie', for example—have become accepted as part of the national heritage, so that many people believe them to be true folk songs.

Scottish song embraces two, if not three, distinct traditions—of the Lowlands, including Border songs much influenced by and mixed up with their English counterparts, and of the Highlands and Islands, which should possibly be regarded as two separate traditions. These groupings are very largely defined by the language of the songs; that of the Lowlands, often referred to as Lallans, may reasonably be regarded as dialect English; that of the others is the Scottish Gaelic, a distinct member of the group of Celtic languages which includes Irish, Welsh, Cornish and Breton.

Ideally, the first category of Scottish song at which we should look is folk song in its purest state—that is, where melody and words originated in some distant past, and were transmitted orally from generation to generation. Even when some of the songs began to be written into the manuscript books of enthusiastic amateurs, and later to be put on permanent record in printed form, such handing down and passing on continued, particularly in rural areas where books were rarities and the ability to read far from widespread. Research in the School of Scottish Studies in the University of Edinburgh has shown that a considerable amount of folk singing in the true sense (that is, for domestic pleasure, not for public exhibition) still persists, and that hitherto unknown folk songs are still occasionally found.

Nevertheless, the nature of modern society is such that these are becoming increasingly rare. The point of actual extinction of folk singing as a spontaneous, indigenous art cannot be very far off.

Convenience, however, suggests a different approach. Scottish National Song emerged from, and exists along with, true folk song, both in the Lowlands and, to a lesser extent, in the Highlands. I shall, therefore, take the two traditions separately, bringing the story of Scottish Lowland song right up to date before considering the songs of the Highlands and Islands.

The preservation of the authentic words of the traditional narrative ballads of Lowland Scotland (which includes the geographically paradoxical areas of much of Aberdeenshire and the coastal areas round the Moray Firth) is primarily due to the Herculean labour of the scholar Francis James Child (1825-96). He collected material from all the printed, MS. and verbal sources he could find and purged them of the romantic additions and 'improvements' of earlier enthusiasts such as Sir Walter Scott. During the 1880s and 90s, Child published, in ten parts, his huge collection of over 300 Scottish and English ballads, most of them in several variant forms. Unlike most earlier editors, Child expressed his awareness that the ballads were originally *sung,* and even published about fifty tunes as an appendix to his great work; but he had neither time nor knowledge to pursue their musical aspect. Certain amateur enthusiasts, notably the father and son Christie in north-east Scotland, collected and published words and music of many ballads. However, their work is vitiated by the then prevailing attitude to folk material, which was to regard it as rustic and untutored, to be 'improved' by alteration, addition and bowdlerisation at editorial discretion; and it is to the monumental work of an American scholar, Bertrand Harris Bronson (b. 22 June 1902) that we owe most of our knowledge of authentic ballad tunes. In four massive volumes (followed by an abbreviated popular single one) Bronson assembled, classified, annotated and published the traditional tunes to which the Child ballads were sung. He is generous in his acknowledgement of the work of predecessors in the field, notably of the Aberdeenshire schoolmaster Gavin Greig (1856-1914), who recorded his labours in collecting ballad poetry and tunes at source in nearly one hundred MS. volumes, much of whose contents were edited by Alexander Keith and first published in 1925.

In a few cases Bronson did not succeed in tracing any tune; but in most he published variant forms from different locations, often running into dozens, and in one case ('Bonny Barbara Allen') to 198. When one considers the nature of the transmission of melodies and words from mouth to ear, it is easy to understand why so many forms exist—memory power and natural musical gift, to take two obvious points, differ in individuals. Anybody is entitled to make subjective judgements and to have preferences for certain versions, but it is both pedantic and logically unsound to maintain that when one variant can be proved to be *older* than another, it is in some way more authentic. As long as oral transmission was a widespread method of communication, *all* variants were authentic.

In a short study it is not practicable to print extracts illustrating the enormous range of emotion and human experience enshrined in the Scottish ballads, still less to give samples of the strength, flexibility and beauty of the melodies to which they were wedded. For these, consult Bronson's works, of which the abridged single volume *The Singing Tradition of Child's Popular Ballads* will satisfy most, and perhaps stimulate others to read the major work. However, some of the finest may be mentioned: the horrific tale of 'The Twa Sisters', one of the best versions of which is Bronson, ballad 10, variant 80; 'Lord Randal' (No. 12); 'The Twa Corbies' (No. 26, variants 8 and 9); 'Thomas Rymer' (No. 30); 'Sir Patrick Spens' (No. 58); 'The Bonny Earl of Murray' (No. 181); 'The Braes of Yarrow' (No. 214). There is an extraordinary strength and concentration in both words and music of these and many other traditional ballads. Much is implied rather than stated; the processes of time and modification over many generations have shorn the poems and tunes of everything superfluous, leaving a granite core of essential material in forms which have survived (as has Handel's *Messiah*) the worst abuse that incompetence and ignorance could heap upon them, through the loving care and unremitting zeal of a limited number of real enthusiasts.

When we consider true folk songs whose main purpose is not narrative but the expression of personal sentiments, it is worth noting that certain versions of some of the ballads in Child's collection have become so shortened and condensed that they may be said to lie on the borderline between balladry and lyricism. Version A of 'The Bonny Earl of Murray' (Child, No. 181), is really a lament for the chief protagonist in a historical drama whose details are assumed to be known to the listener. Similarly, version A of 'Willy Drown'd in Yarrow' (No. 125) is a short poignant expression of personal grief.

Several factors have contributed to our relative ignorance of early records of song (as a marriage of words and music) compared with our fuller knowledge of the ballad. Their very lack of drama would make individual specimens more ephemeral and easily forgotten; their frequent ribaldry and bawdiness would tend to limit circulation; their habit of dwelling upon localised and domestic affairs would confine appeal compared with the universality of the ballad. Not least important, systematic fieldwork in seeking out and setting down original words and tunes without so-called improvement lacked a properly equipped enthusiast such as Child until a great deal of material had been lost. Fortunately recent collectors, notably in connection with the School of Scottish Studies, have saved, and continue to save, much of the considerable remnants from oblivion, as the practice of oral transmission nears extinction.

On the other hand, the seventeenth- and eighteenth-century habit of making collections of tunes *or* words (but rarely both at once) did provide a basis upon which later poets and musicians set to work to build up the corpus of what is called Scots Song. But more of that later.

The earliest and most important of the known surviving MSS., the Skene MS., is believed to date from *c*.1615. As with most of the other MSS.—about a score in all—it was built up for domestic use, and thus puts on record the personal tastes of its compiler. These were to a considerable extent the currently fashionable songs of English composers like John Dowland, but the Skene MS. also contains the melodies and names of a good many Scottish airs, and so establishes proof of their antiquity. Of the surviving MSS., the Skene was studied earlier than any other, its contents having been described by William Dauney in 1838. Most of the others have had to wait until fairly recent times, when scholars like Harry M. Willsher made their contents known to the public. Between them, the MSS. establish the antiquity of a fairly large number of folk-tunes, including 'John Anderson My Jo', 'Tweedside', 'Green Grow the Rashes', 'Bessie Bell' and 'The Flowers of the Forest'. The airs in all these MSS. were written for various instruments, without words, though the first line of the lyric is usually given as a title.

Scottish MSS. containing vocal music as such are almost entirely confined to the works of English composers of their day, and to anonymous settings of words by old Scottish poets in a similar sophisticated style. They cannot, therefore, be classed as folk material—though they are of interest in their own right (see pages 40-1).

In 1650 the London publisher John Playford issued *The English Dancing Master,* a collection of tunes arranged for the fiddle. This became so popular that over several decades more than twenty editions were published, and it included a few old Scottish tunes. Where did Playford find them? It is reasonable to surmise that Scottish musicians and dancing masters who went to London in the wake of the Stuart kings took these tunes with them, and that some became sufficiently popular and widely known to merit inclusion in Playford's work. Indeed, during the reigns of Charles II and James II, the first of the waves of enthusiasm in London for

'Scotch music' encouraged leading composers to include imitations or genuine arrangements among their instrumental works. For example, in his *Apollo's Banquet*, Playford published 'A New Scotch Tune' by Henry Purcell, which is a harpsichord arrangement of an old air whose original words are lost, known to us as 'Peggy I Must Love Thee'. Purcell also included 'Scotch tunes' in his overtures to Shadwell's version of *Timon of Athens* (!) and Dryden's *Amphytrion*, but these seem to be imitations of what was conceived to be the Scottish style. The increasing demand in London for 'Scotch tunes' must have continued, for the Playfords, father and son, included several in subsequent publications, culminating in 1700 in *A Collection of Original Scotch Tunes for the Violin*, which includes many airs familiar today. Later, Burns added or adapted lyrics to most of them.

From the eighteenth century onwards there issued from the presses an ever increasing number of volumes of Scottish traditional tunes, sometimes mixed with newly composed imitations. Most are for fiddle with or without a crude bass, and the majority are clearly intended as dance music. At the outset, these volumes were published mainly in London, but as the century progressed, Edinburgh and Glasgow publishers began to produce collections to meet what was obviously a considerable demand. Many were published anonymously. Others bear the names of their compilers such as Adam Craig, William McGibbon, Alexander McGlashan and James Oswald, whose most famous collection, *The Caledonian Pocket Companion*, was issued in twelve parts in mid-century; it contains hundreds of tunes for the violin, with variations—in the technical sense. This collection was a principal basis for Robert Burns's work, and indeed remains to this day an important source book. The many volumes issued by Niel Gow and his sons up to about 1820 end the list of seventeenth- and eighteenth-century collections of tunes, most of which contain, besides Lowland airs, much Highland material. The nineteenth- and early twentieth-century flood of good, bad and (mostly) indifferent collections, are little more than reprints or cribs of selections from the works already mentioned.

But what of the traditional words? This issue was confused as early as 1718 when the poet Allan Ramsay, no doubt sensing a developing market, issued a small volume of old and new poems to be sung to specified and presumably well-known tunes. Its success prompted Ramsay six years later to bring out a much larger anthology which he called *The Tea-table Miscellany*; to subsequent editions Ramsay added new material totalling almost 500 poems, and its acceptability may be gauged from the fact that, in all, some thirty editions were issued during and after the poet's lifetime. The trouble is that *The Tea-table Miscellany* consists in part of poems by Ramsay himself, with others by certain anonymous 'ingenious young men', and 'such old verses as have been done time out of mind . . .'. Ramsay did not scruple, as regards the last class, to alter, and to add material of his own with the stated intention of rendering them fit for polite society. The quality of Ramsay's additions varies from acceptable to abysmal, but their widespread adoption by later editors has made the task of modern scholars much harder, and almost certainly has meant the passing into limbo of much vigorous genuine traditional material.

In 1769 and 1776 David Herd, a notable enthusiast who was born in Kincardineshire, issued volumes of Scottish songs and ballads which swept Europe with their nicely timed appeal to the rising tide of Romanticism. Again, alas, no music, but a faithfulness to textual origins which did much to counter the damage done by Ramsay's tamperings. We need not concern ourselves with Part I of Herd's work, which has been superseded by that of a number of scholars, culminating in Child; but Parts II and III, containing love songs and humorous songs respectively, are of first-class importance in establishing good texts of a large mass of old Scottish lyric verse.

This survey of origins and early publications must conclude with some consideration of the first books which contain both words and music of Lowland Scottish song. The popularity of Scottish tunes in late seventeenth-century

B

London society clearly broadened into a liking for verse that was, or purported to be, Scottish in character, particularly when it was humorous or satirical. Readers evidently liked to think of the Scots as uncouth and having bumpkinish manners. Thomas D'Urfey catered for this taste with his *Pills to Purge Melancholy*, which includes among its hundreds of songs many 'Scotch tunes', most of them genuine enough, and probably taken from Playford. When it comes to 'Scotch verses', however, the matter is different; almost without exception they are manifestly the work of hacks with what seem to us very odd notions of Scottish manners, dialect and accent, but which presumably were accepted by D'Urfey's readers as the real thing. A very small number of genuine old works is found in *Pills*; for instance, 'Jockey Met with Jenny Fair', altered later by Ramsay, and 'Where Got'st Thou the Haver-mill Bonack' the first couplet of which Burns adapted as the opening of an otherwise original song.

The popularity of successive editions of D'Urfey's *Pills* and of Ramsay's *Tea-table Miscellany* indicates a lively market for Scottish songs in London, and in 1725 an astute singer named William Thomson (not to be confused with George Thomson, of whom more later) produced a volume of fifty songs with their melodies, and with words mostly lifted straight from *The Tea-table Miscellany* without acknowledgement. Each song was given a bass part so that it could be performed with instrumental accompaniment; these basses are obviously the work of somebody who knew his job, and imply harmonies much more sensitive and musicianly than those added by most subsequent editors. Thomson called his work *Orpheus Caledonius* taking his cue from Playford's phenomenally successful *Orpheus Britannicus*. It was a great commercial hit, so much so that Thomson issued a second edition (still giving no credit to Ramsay) in which the number of songs was doubled. Ramsay, not unnaturally, was furious, and made his feelings clear in the preface to the second edition of *The Tea-table Miscellany*. He decided to fight Thomson on his own ground, and was so ill-advised as to issue a volume of *Musick for the Scots Songs in The Tea-table*

Miscellany. It gave *tunes only*, and was full of gross errors of engraving. These circumstances, and its publication in Edinburgh, were no doubt responsible for the venture's failure, and copies are now extremely rare compared with *Orpheus Caledonius*.

William Thomson has been blamed for allowing the prevailing Italian operatic style to influence his presentation of the simple melodies, but examination of the work does not support the criticism. Such modest ornamentation as there is reflects no more than contemporary taste, and is a good deal less objectionable than some later fashions. The manner of presentation and of singing popular songs changes from one generation to another, and in its small way is a comment on the thoughts and feelings of its times.

All in all, *Orpheus Caledonius* fully justifies its claim to be regarded as the first commendable collection of Scottish song, despite the gulf which separates it from what is nowadays regarded as folk song.

After *Orpheus Caledonius* there appeared before the end of the eighteenth century some two dozen collections consisting in whole or in part of Scottish songs with both words and music. Two of these form the subject of my next section. Of the remainder—most of which came into existence by a process analogous to cannibalism—only one merits particular mention in this survey. This is Joseph Ritson's *Scotish* (sic) *Songs,* published in 1794. Every commentator mentions Ritson, usually with respect, but none that I know of has done justice to his scrupulous scholarship and his excellent presentation of a large body of Scottish song, much of it traditional. Perhaps this has something to do with Ritson being an Englishman, an eccentric, and a notoriously ill-tempered (though not unfair) critic of the work of others. Perhaps, too, because his work had the ill luck to appear just as another and greater monument was being erected, its merits were overlooked. Be that as it may, Ritson's musical texts are clean and accurate (his literary ones perhaps a little less so); admittedly, most of the contents are taken from earlier printed works, but Ritson was careful to give precise citations of all his sources. Above all, the work opens with a long and invaluable essay, which is compulsory reading for any serious student of the subject, even though later research has shown that some of Ritson's conclusions were erroneous.

Millions of words, in countless thousands of books, essays, lectures and speeches, have been devoted to the works of the Scottish poet Robert Burns, and I have no wish to add more than are absolutely necessary. The basic fact is that Burns (1759-96) was a man of peasant stock with a gift for lyrical expression which at its best amounts to genius. He was intensely affected by the liberal ideas spreading through much of Europe at that time, and felt passionately about the rights of man, and man's essential nobility. What concerns us here is not his extraordinary gift for satirical comment on political and religious hypocrisy, but the consuming passion for the speech and song of his native Lowland Scotland which caused him to devote his last years almost exclusively, and entirely altruistically, to preserving and perpetuating as much of it as he could lay hands on.

Burns's gifts included a strong natural ear for music, certainly for the traditional native product. I stress this because it has often been denied, overlooked or belittled by people who should have known better. In all, Burns produced for publication some 350 lyric poems *to be sung* to known Scottish airs, usually chosen by himself and specified by title. Some of the poems were entirely of his own composition; some were reconstructions of fragmentary or imperfect old songs, and some were virtually untouched original folk material.

Burns wrote or adapted poems in Lowland Scottish and in English. On the whole, he is at his best in the vernacular, with such immortal songs as 'O Wert Thou in the Cauld Blast', 'Ye Banks and Braes o' Bonnie Doon' and 'The Deil's Awa wi' th' Exciseman'. It is certainly true that we find his least felicitous efforts among his English songs, but surprisingly few are really bad, and most of those were written in response to outside pressure. Probably one-fifth of his songs, in their marriage to lovely tunes, are masterpieces.

It is doubtful if Schubert attained so high a proportion.

Circumstances brought Burns into contact with two men, each of whom had a scheme for publication of a large collection of the national music of Great Britain. They were James Johnson, a comparatively humble Edinburgh publisher, and George Thomson, a civil servant who combined undoubted enthusiasm with prudery and the arrogance sometimes found in amateurs in their dealings with professionals.

Johnson had collected a good deal of material for his first volume when Burns came on the scene and in effect took over the editorship. The scheme was modified to exclude almost all but Scottish songs, and eventually, under the title *The Scots Musical Museum*, reached six volumes of 100 songs each, though Burns did not live to see its completion. Burns himself contributed about a quarter of the lyrics and named the tunes to which they should be sung. In the case of poems from other authors, he normally chose the version of the stipulated air, sometimes using tunes which he had heard and remembered, sometimes referring to printed sources — notably Oswald's *Caledonian Pocket Companion* — but occasionally deciding on, or recommending, tunes printed in other collections. It is a pity that Burns pointedly disavowed understanding of the more sophisticated aspects of musical technique, for it is a weakness of *The Scots Musical Museum* that the accompaniments, which were the work of a local musician named Stephen Clark and his son, are at best rather dull, and at worst show signs of laziness and indifference; however, this aspect of the *Museum* is easily ignored. The collection at once became, and has remained ever since, the principal source book of Scottish National Song. It includes much of Burns's best work in the field.

As for George Thomson's elephantine *magnum opus*, it must be said at once that but for the fact it was the means of bringing into the world several more of Burns's finest creations, it can only be regarded as a joke. The egregious Thomson had the idea that the vulgar and bucolic native product should be cleaned up and made fit for the ears of 'the fair sex' among the middle and upper classes in Edinburgh's fast-growing New Town. He therefore had no compunction about making unauthorised alterations to the work of the poets who wrote for him, choosing unsuitable tunes against Burns's wishes, and in general behaving as an arrogant meddler. Thomson also had the absurd idea of employing Continental composers such as Beethoven, Haydn and Pleyel to write introductions and accompaniments, with results so ludicrous that one can listen to them only with a mixture of laughter, tears and rage. This does not prevent solemn Teutonic lieder-singers from including them occasionally in programmes intended to be serious. The huge, pretentious volumes of Thomson's *Select Collection of Original Scottish Airs* are a sad memorial to misplaced enthusiasm and ignorant amateurishness. Even so, but for Thomson, and Burns's acceptance of much that enraged him (as some of his letters make clear), we should be the poorer for the loss of some immortal Scottish lyrics. Burns's work on both collections was done purely for love and virtually without thought of financial reward.

Following *The Scots Musical Museum*, the nineteenth and twentieth centuries brought a flood of collections of Scottish songs—good, bad, indifferent or shaming as to presentation and musical arrangements. Not surprisingly, their contents are to a great extent culled from Johnson's and Thomson's works, with a gradual accumulation of additional material, genuine and spurious. The musical accompaniments and settings inevitably reflect the fashions of their day, and in this respect what was acceptable to one generation became outmoded to the next. For example, the rich romanticism of Hamish McCunn's accomplished settings gave way to the musicianly competence of editors like Alfred Moffat, and they in their turn to the comparatively sparse arrangements of *The Oxford Scottish Song Book*. Perhaps the most important collection since *The Scots Musical Museum* was George Farquhar Graham's *The Songs of Scotland* (1848-9), valuable for the editor's voluminous commentaries but, alas, rather spoiled by pianoforte accompaniments which at times display misguided ingenuity, and at others sheer insensitivity and even incompetence.

Following Burns, minor poets like Allan Cunningham and James Hogg, and a host of smaller fry, continued to write verses to be sung to named Scottish tunes, and a number of these have, as it were, been accepted into the canon. Examples are, 'My Love She's but a Lassie Yet' and 'A Wee Bird Cam to our Ha' Door'.

The nineteenth century also saw the development of another kind of song, of which some early examples like 'Caller Herring' and 'Annie Laurie' have taken their places beside much-loved older material. In these, neither words nor music were venerable, and in some cases were the work of one person. The growing custom among the Victorian middle classes of spending the evening singing in each other's drawing-rooms began to call forth a flood of songs whose words were in what their authors fondly imagined to be Scottish dialect, and whose music (often the work of Englishmen or Irishmen) is impossible to distinguish from the Victorian drawing-room ballad style. The growing sentimentality of the age, and the development of the misty-mountains-and-heather conception of a Scotland in which Lowlands, Highlands and Islands were merged in a preposterous romantic image, produced a legion of hacks who churned out nostalgic ditties like 'A Guid New Year to Ane and A' and 'Bonnie Galloway', spurious love songs such as 'Bonny Mary of Argyle' and 'The Bonny Lass of Ballochmyle', and uncountable masses of shaming ballads which were often banal in the last degree. Worst of all, some of the songs which Burns had written to glorious native tunes were forced from their natural settings and allied to newly composed melodies. Among the best-known of these is 'Flow Gently Sweet Afton', and it is a matter for shame that the Scots for so long accepted Alexander Hume's saccharine substitute for the gorgeous original tune selected by the poet himself. It is difficult to describe or explain adequately the degeneracy into which the Scots allowed their heritage to sink, and it is for social historians rather than musicians to explain the enthusiasm with which many Scots, today, greet the barrage of sentimental slush about misty islands and wee heather-covered cottages on countless gramophone records and broadcasts. Part of the blame must be laid at the door of a misguided genius named Harry Lauder, who encapsulated the English escapist conception of the Scots in a long series of couthy tusheries; even so, it remains a mystery to me that a so-called proud nation can accept and apparently enjoy this cartoon of themselves — and worse — as they are depicted in musical plays and films of transatlantic origin which shall remain nameless, as they deserve.

Fortunately, there is another side to the contemporary picture. Thanks to a number of devoted amateur enthusiasts, whose work was later channelled into the systematic research of the School of Scottish Studies, a great deal of material has been retrieved; and through dedication of talented singers, professional and amateur, who have specialised in Scottish folk song, a great deal of it has become popular. This acts as a counterbalance to the commercial exploitation of the insincere and nostalgic phoney-folkery. In particular, the use of the guitar as an accompanying instrument, so far from being a modern nonsense, is a return to a custom which was common enough in earlier days. It is, of course, all too easy to play the guitar badly; but good players have encouraged a style of accompaniment which has helped to revive interest and pleasure in the performance of genuine Scottish National Song.

VOCAL MUSIC IN THE HIGHLANDS AND ISLANDS

Two related factors dictated that the folk music of the Highlands and Islands should develop its distinct individuality and styles quite differently from those of the Lowlands. These were geography and language.

In the days before the extensive building of roads and of

easy transport, the remoteness and difficulty of access to the Highlands, and still more to the islands, isolated their inhabitants, dividing them into clans—whose supposed tartans nowadays make such a brave show at parades in Princes Street and at Highland Gatherings—who waged incessant internecine warfare in the struggle for existence in a hostile environment. The language of those parts, which is now itself fighting a rearguard action in the face of modern communications, was Scottish Gaelic, one of the group of languages evolved by the Celtic races in the extreme west of Europe.

It is true that the very few who passed between the Highlands and Lowlands, such as cattle drovers and soldiers on punitive expeditions, did carry back and forward the occasional tune which might be used as the musical basis for a new song in the other language, and this accounts for such limited interchange of music as can be detected. The difference of language virtually excluded the possibility of interchange of words, and it was thus inevitable that each region would accumulate a store of folk poetry related to its own activities and interests.

Moreover, the indigenous music of the Highlands, and still more that of the islands, existed (and still does to a limited extent) in the oral tradition for much longer than that of the Lowlands, again for geographical reasons. Even today, when aeroplanes and car-ferries have greatly reduced the physical effort of reaching Lewis, Barra and the like, a visit to smaller outer islands such as Vatersay or Eriskay is quite a formidable undertaking. The continuing effect of depopulation, and of radio and television, must be blamed for the fact that the Highland folk tradition—like that of the Lowlands—is doomed, to be preserved only by the conscious efforts of professional ethnologists aided by enthusiastic collectors of folk material, and by singers who perpetuate some of the songs as a worthwhile and profitable way of filling people's leisure time.

The songs of the Highlands (which for convenience I shall take to include those of the islands) naturally reflect the life style of succeeding generations of Highlanders. They fall into two broad divisions—the heroic and the domestic—corresponding roughly to the balladry and lyric folk song of the Lowlands. Each class can be subdivided almost indefinitely, and much has been written on the subject by authors whose outlooks vary enormously—from dreary academicism to Celtic Twilight Romanticism, with many degrees of competence between.

The great heroic songs were composed by professional bards who, if legend is to be believed, underwent a training of almost unbelievable rigour; some of their names are known, and around their personalities has grown a folklore nearly as extensive as their poetical works. These works describing the merits, deeds and deaths of legendary Celtic heroes of antiquity, have no doubt some remote basis in historical fact, but they have in the course of time accumulated masses of figmentary detail. All were intended to be sung (some believe to the accompaniment of the *clàrsach*, an elementary type of harp). Although the last of them can be dated as far back as the fourteenth century, versions were alive as late as the early twentieth century (such is the incredible tenacity of the Highland folk memory). They were sung to various old tunes which are certainly not the originals—sometimes to more than one tune for different variants of the same ballad.

It is odd that the next roughly datable folk material of the Highlands comes after a lapse of hundreds of years, from the seventeenth century. Again from known poets, both male and female, again written to known tunes, again dealing with manly subjects, they now refer not to the heroes of Celtic legend, but to ascertainable personages and historic events. Praise of the individual merits and military valour of notable clan chieftains and laments for their deaths were favourite topics; the heroes of such poems were often, it must be said, the patrons or employers of the poets in question. These 'great songs' *(orain mhor)* occupy a special place in the affections of Scottish Gaels today; competitors for the highest awards at the annual assembly *(mod)* of the Highland

Society *(An comunn Gaidhealach)* are required, among other tests, to prove excellence in ability to sing them.

We shall see later that the repertoire of the Scottish bagpipe is divided into 'great' and 'little' music. Somewhat similarly, Gaelic song separates into the 'great music' described above, and lesser music, consisting of songs related to the events of everyday life. The Highlander found a song for every occasion, be it his work, his love affairs, his homeland, the works of nature, weddings, funerals, fights, putting the baby to sleep, or merely passing an idle hour by setting the rhythm for dancing. In general, these songs conform more closely to the accepted definition of folk song than do the 'great songs' and ballads, since both their verbal and musical origins are anonymous, whereas at least the words of ballads and 'great songs' can be ascribed to a known poet. Some can be grouped as specific types, of which the largest is probably the labour songs, designed either to synchronise the movements of several people engaged in a communal task, or to lighten monotony, or both.

Today, many of the labour songs are associated with 'waulking', or tweed-shrinking, an important element in the economy of the islands, and a prolonged and monotonous operation which required women working together. Apart from gossip, it was the custom to reduce the tedium by singing rhythmic songs in which solo and chorus alternated, often with great rapidity. The strong accents of the songs accompanied the heavy thumping of the wet tweed on a board. It is clear to me that the suitability of this particular combination of work and song for public exhibitions of 'folk customs' has narrowed it into a channel which suggests a clearer-cut 'type' of song than was actually the case; every community must have had its own favourite songs, and used the rhythmically suitable ones during the waulking process, whether or not the songs had a specific alliance to waulking.

Waulking as a genuine activity lasted well into the twentieth century. Not so rowing in work crews—an equally monotonous occupation calling for synchronisation of movement, with which a large body of strongly rhythmic song is associated. Again I must stress that there is little evidence to support the romantic notion of a big corpus of song *exclusively* used to accompany rowing. Few, if any, of the verses of such songs make any reference to rowing, and Francis Collinson tells us that many songs are common to rowing and waulking, which supports my view that too much has been made of the idea that specific communal tasks called for specific types of song.

A more recognisable type is the lullaby (though many of these too were used in other labour contexts); Gaelic folk song is particularly rich in beautiful songs associated with the business of putting babies to sleep (and so giving mother a littel peace). The justly famous *Griogal Cridhe*, one of the loveliest melodies in the world, and one of the most maltreated by 'arrangers', combines its functional purpose with genuine pathos in its words expressing grief at the tragic death of the child's father.

One of the most frequently found types of Gaelic song (I hesitate to call it a group) is that which nostalgically recalls the singer's homeland. Many of the best of these originated in the Clearances of the eighteenth and nineteenth centuries, when untold numbers of islanders and Highlanders were forcibly removed from their native districts, most of them emigrating to Canada, the U.S.A. and elsewhere. Scarcely an island, region or even mountain but has its songs of praise and longing. This has been a rich field for composers and poets of later date, who have sometimes added to the repertoire with remarkable success, as in the well-known *An t' Eilean Muilach (The Isle of Mull)*. Lamentably, it must be said, it has also given rise to a great deal of rubbish produced for commercial exploitation of man's natural sentimentality.

It is not possible here to deal individually with every type of Gaelic song—the feelings of successful or disappointed lovers, the eulogies and laments, the purely comic song, the sung dance music known as *port-a-beul*, and all the rest; but a word or two must be said about the *ceilidh*. The real meaning of the word has become blurred by its use in public gatherings and broadcasts, as meaning something indistinguishable from a concert, sometimes with a few exhibition dances thrown in. Perhaps *An comunn Gaidhealach* bears some responsibility for the transition from the original meaning— a gathering of friends and neighbours to pass the evening, and often a good part of the night, in entertaining one another with song, poetry and story. It is in the nature of things that at each annual national *mod*, the organisers should arrange for *ceilidhs* to which the public is invited on payment, as part of the celebrations. On these occasions, however, visiting choirs and groups, as well as random gatherings of a few individuals, tend to hold their own more or less spontaneous *ceilidhs* in hotel rooms and private premises, and these are perhaps a greater justification of the *mod* than the formal singing competitions. The most usual form taken by the songs at a *ceilidh* is for each to open with a chorus, after which the individual singer alternates verses with repetitions of the same chorus, sung by all.

The study of Gaelic song has been confused by the circumstances in which much of it was saved from oblivion, and it is fashionable nowadays to blame Marjory Kennedy-Fraser and her literary collaborator Kenneth Macleod for this state of affairs. Mrs Kennedy-Fraser (1857-1930) was a Scottish singer who developed a passion for collecting folk songs, particularly in the Hebridean islands. She arranged and published a large number and made them famous by singing them all over the world. The appeal of her work, particularly to Scots at home and in exile, was phenomenal in her time, and to some extent remains to this day. But for her work much Gaelic folk song would by now be lost beyond recall, and she can scarcely be blamed for living at a time when not only was Romanticism well into its final stage of decay, but before tape-recorders and before modern methods of studying and editing folk material evolved. Mrs Kennedy-Fraser, with a devotion to her task matched by the physical discomforts involved in carrying it out, put on record a great mass of material from the Scottish islands by writing it down as nearly accurately as she could, or by recording it on an extremely unreliable old clockwork cylinder machine. Her literary collaborator transcribed texts, amended them or wrote new ones; this, after all, was only what Burns had done with Lowland folk song, though with rather more genius and sense of fitness. It can be regretted, even if not condemned, that the social climate in which Mrs Kennedy-Fraser lived virtually *demanded* that she present her work in an aura of Celtic Twilight and whimsy, with harmonies and pianoforte accompaniments which, however acceptable in 1909, are now felt to be inept. Her published versions of the songs, moreover, involved the strait-jacketing of their subtly varied and often complex rhythms into the conventional bar-structure of European musical orthodoxy. However, she left on record much of what she originally heard, to the great advantage of scholars whose studies are based on the scientific collecting and recording methods developed by people like Bartók and Kodaly in Eastern Europe. What is not easy to forgive is the continuation of Mrs Kennedy-Fraser's style of presentation by others whose knowledge and techniques were inferior to her own, whose attitudes tended to degenerate into revolting sentimentality, and whose motives for publication were decidedly less altruistic.

Space does not allow for discussion of the work of such devoted collectors as Frances Tolmie or Father Allan MacDonald, or of the scholars John Lorne Campbell and Francis Collinson, which is easily accessible to those who wish to go deeper into the subject. As with Lowland song, the School of Scottish Studies is closely involved in preserving for posterity as much of the heritage of the Highlands and Islands as can be saved, and we must be grateful that so much *has* been saved, in however imperfect a state some of it may be, before it was too late.

INSTRUMENTAL MUSIC

To multitudes of people the world over, the Scottish nation is symbolised by the sound of the great Highland bagpipe;

indeed, I would guess that most native Scots believe that there is no other national instrumental music worth considering. Many a fiddler from Shetland or Strathspey could prove otherwise, and a smaller but no less dedicated band of enthusiasts could remind them of the claims of the *clàrsach,* or Celtic harp, to have the longest and most honourable ancestry of all.

The Clàrsach. It is proved that there were harps and harpers in Scotland in the early Middle Ages, because they appear on certain stone carvings, of which one at least dates from the ninth century; but what they played, and whether it was accompaniment to ballads or purely instrumental, is conjectural. The romantic element in all of us tends to assume that the bards used the music of the *clàrsach* as a background to their singing, and no doubt this was true not only in Scotland, but also in Ireland and Wales, where the harp's history is at least as venerable; but there are several references by sixteenth-century writers to the harp, some of which suggest that its music went beyond the needs of vocal accompaniment. Collinson quotes mention of harpers in domestic account books and so on, from which it can be taken that some establishments included a harper among the servants. It is surely stretching credulity too far to suppose that these harpers were kept for the purpose of accompanying visiting singers — think of the rehearsal problems! On the other hand, it remains just possible that the term 'harper' had a less precise meaning than we give it today, and that it meant one who sang to his own harp accompaniment.

Employment of private harpers was not unusual at one time, but they seem to have become fewer and fewer until, about the mid-eighteenth century, the harp and its music disappeared altogether from the Scottish scene.

By great good fortune, two fifteenth- or sixteenth-century *clàrsachs* were preserved, in excellent condition, and eventually presented to the Scottish Museum of Antiquities in Edinburgh, where they may be seen today. Thus, when an attempt was made to revive interest in the 'Scottish harp' at the end of the nineteenth century, models were available to provide a basis for the design of new instruments. Even so, nothing might have come of it but for Mrs Kennedy-Fraser's daughter who adopted the *clàrsach* to accompany her own singing of Hebridean airs on her world-wide concert tours. As none of the music played by the old harpers has survived, the whole present-day repertoire of the instrument consists of music composed during the twentieth century. There is plenty of scope for the same kind of musical amateurishness as is found in too much of today's guitar accompaniment to Scottish songs, as well as for a particular kind of Celtic-Twilight coyness. Nevertheless, as a number of real artists like the late Jean Campbell demonstrated, the *clàrsach* can be skilfully and effectively used in public and private music-making. Its revival, or rather its renaissance, and the continuing modest increase in the number of its devotees, are welcomed as a significant addition to the Scottish means of self-expression.

The Scottish Fiddle. Anybody who saw the television programme in which Yehudi Menuhin joined a band of Scottish traditional fiddlers at Blair Castle and exchanged technical know-how with their leader will be aware that fiddling is very much a live, popular art in Scotland. This is particularly true of certain parts of the country such as Strathspey and Shetland, whose styles of playing show considerable and significant differences. Flourishing societies, where solo and concerted fiddling are practised, exist in many centres, and have large followings for their specialised repertoire. This consists to a great extent of Scottish airs with variations, and national dance music, played in a style developed by the many fiddle player-composers of the eighteenth and early nineteenth centuries.

We read of Scottish players of rebecks and pre-Amati violins in the sixteenth century, particularly of the band who serenaded Mary, Queen of Scots, at Holyrood Palace, where it is said that the queen thanked them and praised their efforts, but moved to a bedroom out of earshot of their demonstrations of loyalty. Important for the future of the art of fiddling in Scotland was the development of the modern instrument by great Italian violin-makers such as the Amati family. Scottish craftsmen copied them, starting a tradition of fiddle-making which persists to this day. Since Scottish-built fiddles can be not only excellent in themselves, but objects of great aesthetic beauty, it is not surprising that the best specimens are highly prized, and regarded by their owners with as much care and affection as if they were Strads.

A few collections of Scottish airs for instrumental (including fiddle) use were published in London in the late seventeenth and early eighteenth centuries and a little later in Edinburgh, some of which included simple melodic variations. But the first volumes containing music specifically designed for the instrument appeared in Edinburgh about the mid-eighteenth century. They contain reels and other dance tunes, and Francis Collinson points out that the 1780 collection issued by Angus Cumming is the first appearance in print of the fiddle music of Strathspey — Cumming himself, a native of Grantown, being its most notable exponent. It would be tedious to name all the fiddle composers who contributed to the repertoire — those who are interested can find them listed in reference books. Mention must be made, though, of one or two of the most influential, of whom the first in point of time was James Oswald. Of his publications, the most voluminous is *The Caledonian Pocket Companion* (they must have had large pockets in those days). It is a compendium of national instrumental music comparable to its vocal equivalent, *The Scots Musical Museum*; indeed, it was one of Burns's principal sources of tunes for the lyrics which he wrote for that and other song books. When Burns wrote his cantata, *The Jolly Beggars*, he included a fiddler in his gang of down-and-outs; but the bagpipe is never mentioned or alluded to in the entire poem.

A little later a native of Perthshire named Niel Gow, and

C

various members of his family, were destined to become the most famous of all Scottish fiddlers. So talented were they that their services were in enormous demand all over Scotland, and in London, as providers of dance music for balls and parties in royal and aristocratic circles. Niel Gow and one of his sons, Nathaniel, added considerably as composers to the repertoire of Scottish fiddle music. Many of their tunes became the basis of songs, some of which have achieved widespread fame and taken their place in song books along with traditional and older material (see page 17).

Thus was built up, by many player-composers, the immense body of Scottish fiddle music which is to be found in printed collections, large and small, of this century, some excellent as to accuracy and presentation, some shoddy and unreliable.

It is heartening to know that the art of fiddling continues to flourish in Scotland, and though the best-known names are those of legendary professional fiddlers like Niel Gow and Scott Skinner, great numbers of amateurs give much pleasure by the practice of this traditional art.

The fiddle music of the Shetland Islands is of a quite distinctive kind, radically different from that of the Scottish mainland, and fascinating in its ethnological implications. In a part of the British Isles where the indigenous literary arts flourish to an extent perhaps unequalled elsewhere, maybe we should not be surprised at the vigour with which the art of fiddling is pursued, or at the quantity of original music which is still being composed by its practitioners. Inevitably, in view of Shetland's historical and geographical connections with Norway, this fiddle music shows Scandinavian influences virtually to the exclusion of Scottish ones. One fears the effect of modern communications and of the exploitation of North Sea oil upon one of the few living musical folk traditions which remain with us; fortunately, there is time to do something about putting Shetland music on record before it is too late.

A good deal of Scottish fiddle music is performed today to

a hideous semi-vamped pianoforte accompaniment. The B.B.C., which might have done much to stamp out the practice, is blameworthy, since it has seemed at times to encourage it. Newcomers to the art of Scottish fiddling, faced with this regrettable watering of the stock, should remember that this is *string* music, and should try to appreciate what the effect would be if the illegitimate background were removed.

The Bagpipe. The bagpipe is almost as old as civilised man, and has existed in various forms all over the world. In some places such as Scotland, Ireland, north-east England, Spain and Yugoslavia, bagpipes are still played; in others the instrument has become extinct, as in Germany and Norway; in still others, like Canada and Pakistan, the bagpipe is an importation based on the Scottish Highland model. In Scotland there were, until quite recently, several different instruments operated on the bagpipe principle, but of these only one survives, the Great Highland Pipe, once the pride of the Highland clans. The great pipe was given a new lease of life, which looks like lasting indefinitely, by its adoption as the official musical instrument of the Scottish regiments in the British Army.

It is impossible to say when, or how, the bagpipe came to Scotland—whether imported from outside or independently evolved. Records in sculpture and literature show that primitive forms of the instrument were in use as early as the opening of the fifteenth century, and, not unexpectedly, folk-tradition has it that it was played at the battle of Bannockburn in 1314. The instrument reached its present form in the eighteenth century, with the addition of the bass drone. It now consists of a bag or air reservoir, a blow-pipe, three drones and a chanter pierced at intervals to produce a scale of nine notes, which differs in vital respects from the diatonic scales of Western music. The most obvious features of the bagpipe scale are that one of its notes (D) is very sharp, and another (G) very flat as compared with the major scale. These differences, incidentally, are a main reason why it is difficult to combine the Highland bagpipe with other instruments, though the Scottish composer Ian Whyte contrived, with considerable success, to do so in his ballet *Donald of the Burthens*. Other attempts have been less fortunate.

The features of the Great Highland Pipe which contribute to its unique sound include the continuous triple drone made by a combination of fundamental notes and harmonics, its loud distinctive quality of tone which is incapable of expression by variation of volume, and the convenient layout of the holes in the chanter which enables the fingers to execute astounding feats of dexterity, and to provide strong agogic accents by means of elaborate grace notes as a substitute for the rhythmic pulse obtainable on other instruments.

It is sad that the musicians of the piping fraternity and those in the wider world of Western musical orthodoxy have come to regard one another with a certain suspicion, as was shown by the delays and difficulties which beset moves to include the bagpipe in the list of instruments acceptable at the music examinations of the Scottish Certificate of Education. Mutual understanding is made more difficult by the use of technical terms such as 'augmented 4th', 'diminished 7th' and 'cadence' by both sides, but with different meanings.

The Great Highland Pipe (which to most people *is* the bagpipe), its fabled practitioners of the past, its music and its influence in the winning of wars, are all the subjects of a vast and complicated mystique, not to say a mythology. Its classical repertory, commonly called *piobaireachd* or pibroch, but more correctly *ceol mor* or big music, has always drawn a small but almost fanatical band of followers, some of whom have at times shown more enthusiasm than knowledge, and a tendency to dogmatise rather than to consider facts objectively. The public at large tends to prefer *ceol beag* or little music, which consists of marches, reels, strathspeys, jigs, and airs. The really knowledgeable accept that there are two kinds of pipe music existing side by side, both of them legitimate, and they have even subdivided *ceol beag* into more and less worthy grades. Fanatics affect to despise any pipe music but *ceol mor,* and spend much of their lives disputing fine points of style and propriety which have little if anything to do with the real art that lies behind them.

The social uses of *ceol beag* early became apparent. In due course there was interchange of repertoire between bagpipe and fiddle; fiddlers adopted dance tunes from the pipes for the fast reel and jig, while the pipers borrowed the fiddlers' slower strathspey, and soon adapted it to their instrument's particular genius. It became the custom in both worlds to couple the dances—a stately strathspey being immediately followed by a lively (and sometimes wild) reel.

As for the use of the pipes in battle, there is something to be said for the perhaps cynical view that their sound instils courage in friend and terror in foe. Leaving aside romantic pictures of feather-bonneted, hairy-sporraned, white-spatted pipers egging the troops on to victory at Abraham's Heights, the spirited sound of pipers and drummers playing a sturdy march must on many occasions have alleviated the tedium and physical tiredness of troops on the march. Nor can it be denied that the symbolic use of pipers at a military tattoo or parade can provide a stirring emotional experience.

As for using background pipe music in films, television and radio to conjure up a Scottish atmosphere, one might wish that producers could think of some tune other than the ubiquitous 'Scotland the Brave'.

The serious business of piping, the playing of *piobaireachd* or *ceol mor* is, however, another matter. *Ceol mor* is essentially a personal expression requiring exceptional technical skills acquired by years of study and practice, and an attitude of dedication comparable to that of a great international conductor or solo performer in the world of music at large. Equal dedication and accumulated understanding of the fine points of the art are called for from the listener, whose emotional reactions must be supported by an appreciation of detail which grows with experience. Above all, acute and sustained concentration over long periods are needed from both player and listener.

It seems to me that these requirements have led to a situation where some experts have lost sight of the spirit of *ceol mor* in their enthusiasm for what they conceive to be its letter. If I am not mistaken, some judges at competitions are more concerned that players should not deviate by one little finger from the precise text laid down by previous pundits, than that they show any sign of originality or personal interpretation of the hereditary canon. Seumas MacNeill, a foremost authority and player of *ceol mor,* deplores this situation in his book on *piobaireachd* when he regretfully refers to the absence, during the nineteenth and twentieth centuries, of any real advance in standards of playing. 'Compositions of worth in the nineteenth century are practically non-existent', he writes, and 'The next generation of pipers not only did not compose—they almost certainly considered that there was a touch of *lèse-majesté* about any attempt to do so.' MacNeill is guardedly more hopeful about the future, and about present-day composers of *ceol mor.*

I think that what happened to classical pipe music is more complicated, and that the present impasse is the inevitable consequence of happenings centuries ago. I believe that classical pipe music originated as one of those folk-forms in which players repeated their tunes as often as they pleased with increasingly intricate *extempore* variations; the style and quality of the variations were a reflection of the talent and personality of the individual, and no two performances of the same piece would ever be identical. When the art had reached a stage of development which justified setting up the famous piping colleges said to have existed in Skye and Ulva and elsewhere, young pipers of talent came under the domination of dogmatic— admittedly highly gifted — masters who not only insisted that pupils copy their every minute movement and nuance, but taught that any deviation must be condemned as a fault. Hence the fixed forms were transmitted down the generations, and an art which had rested essentially on extemporisation became frozen in the forms set down by certain strong-minded individuals. The printing of these forms reinforced their sanctity, and before long the immutable principles upon which they were founded acquired a status akin to that of the Bible.

MacNeill appears to support this view when he reports the legend that when a MacCrimmon pupil extemporised embellishments more elaborate than any before, 'Patrick Og MacCrimmon felt that things had gone too far, and *eliminated some of them*' (author's italics). This was in 1730, when Patrick Og was in charge of the fabled piping college at Boreraig in Skye; it would be ungracious to suggest that the great master might have seen in his gifted pupil a threat to his status as the world's leading player.

It is significant that in Scotland an analogous art developed in the vocal embellishment of simple psalm tunes (see pages 37-8). Extempore melodic variation is an art as old as music itself, and is a characteristic of folk music the world over. *Ceol mor* must at one time have been a supremely subtle example of this art, and circumstances channelled it into a fixed course from which enlightened pipers like Seumas MacNeill are now attempting to free it. I have no doubt that there will be much opposition from the old guard of pipers, both in and out of the Army, to any broadening of the art's base—which may be a subconscious expression of the professional's antagonism to the highly knowledgeable amateur.

Only very few people will be willing, or able, to make the effort required to appreciate a good performance of a *piobaireachd* such as the 'Lament for Donald ban', but those who do will be well rewarded.

Music of the Church in Scotland

Before the Reformation

There is a good deal of evidence that quite elaborate musical establishments existed at certain times in pre-Reformation Scotland, notably under King James IV, whose Chapel Royal at Stirling employed, soon after 1500, nearly forty men and boy singers. Almost all copies of the music sung in such places were destroyed under the pretext of religious zeal by the mobs who sacked and pillaged ecclesiastical buildings during the Reformation. It is just possible that Scotland lost the evidence of a notable school of native composers in consequence.

By the greatest good fortune, two MSS. escaped the holocaust, one dubiously associated with Dunkeld, and the other, more significant one, with Scone Abbey; both are preserved in Edinburgh.

The Scone MS. contains over a score of compositions; some are anonymous, some are copies of recognised works by English and Flemish composers. For our purposes its importance is that it establishes Robert Carver, a Scot, as the author of seven big-scale church compositions. Some of these pieces have been published in modern editions, which show that Carver was no run-of-the-mill monkish musician, but a composer of great imagination and immense technical accomplishment. His most spectacular piece is the motet 'O Bone Jesu', composed for no fewer than nineteen solo voices. Carver was acutely inspired by his verbal texts, and there are several miraculous moments when all nineteen voices join in incredibly rich, colourful, romantic illustration of the word Jesu with a series of evocative adjectives culminating in 'O amantissime Jesu, O desideratissime Jesu, O mitissime Jesu . . .'. There can be few instances where a composer's imagination has been carried to such ecstatic heights by the impact of single words.

Several sixteenth-century composers followed Carver with compositions for ecclesiastical use which show technical skill and, occasionally, some aesthetic inspiration; but they were big fishes in a little pond. Carver alone among Scottish composers of the Renaissance bears comparison as a creative artist with the giants of the English, Flemish and Italian schools.

AFTER THE REFORMATION

The chance that the Reformation would bring to light any composers of music for the church in Scotland was obliterated by the very nature of the Reformation. It is easy to oversimplify the immense complexities of the religious struggles which led to, and followed, Martin Luther's famous gesture in 1517; but it is broadly true that in the parts of Europe which followed Luther's dogmatic lead, music flourished as an integral part of liturgical practice, and called forth a long string of composers of the first importance, culminating in J. S. Bach. In countries which accepted the sterner precepts of Zwingli and Calvin, any but the simplest of musical settings came to be frowned on as worldly distractions.

The leading figure of the Reformation in Scotland was John Knox, who had a profound belief in Calvin's principles and an overwhelming determination to apply them in his own country. Knox was a good deal more broad-minded than is often supposed, but he was followed by disciples who carried the dogma they developed from Knox's and Calvin's teachings to fanatic lengths which ensured that church music was restricted to a few plain settings of the psalms in metrical paraphrase. No instrumental accompaniment was permitted, and a curious aspect of the Scottish reformers' zeal is what Kenneth Elliott has described as an almost pathological hatred of the organ. They encouraged—even supervised—the destruction of virtually every organ in the country.

This is not the place to discuss the factional strife which, almost (am I right in saying almost?) to the present day, has characterised Scottish religious life in the country as a whole and in its individual communities. Sectarian disjunctions and conjunctions so complicated that only specialists can follow them, never mind understand them, may offer a commentary on the Scottish character; but they have seen to it that no opportunity for sowing the seed, let alone reaping the harvest, of anything that could be described as a field of Scottish church music has occurred since the Reformation. It is ironic that one or two splendid anthems by twentieth-century Scottish composers are in the regular repertory of choirs in cathedrals and large parish churches in England, but are seldom heard at home. Moreover, one of the finest settings of the Ordinary of the Mass composed this century is from the pen of an English Protestant, Kenneth Leighton, a long-term resident of Edinburgh.

As with the 'Auld Scots Sangs', there still exists in the minds of some, mostly elderly, Scots a vague romantic hankering after the 'Old Scottish Psalm Tunes'. This is no bad thing, since many of the tunes are very fine in their limited way. But a little research into twentieth century Scottish books of church praise reveals that some favourites, like 'Belmont' and 'Crimond', are not even as old as Queen Victoria, and that very, very few of them have any claim to be Scottish, but come from Genevan, French, German and other sources. A large proportion of the 'Old Scottish Psalm Tunes' are eighteenth-century English compositions, while a few are rather poor adaptations of tunes by Beethoven, Mendelssohn and Spohr in the nineteenth century.

Take away all those tunes, however fine, which only custom and nostalgia can regard as being 'Old Scottish', and we are left with a tiny residue of psalm tunes, some (but not all) with Scottish names. Within their restricted scope, some have a strength and rugged beauty fully equal to any adaptations from abroad—'Martyrs', 'Elgin', 'Wigtown', 'Culross' and 'York' are tunes that any nation might be proud of. There are only two flies in the ointment—nobody has proved that they are Scottish in origin (or that they are not), and hardly anybody, even among Scottish church-goers, knows them.

I cannot leave the subject of church music without referring to one aspect which, so far as I know, has not yet been thoroughly explored or documented. I mentioned earlier the effect on their folk music of the remoteness and inaccessibility of parts of the Highlands, and particularly of the outer islands. One result of this remoteness has been the flourishing of extreme Calvinist views in certain parts of the Highlands. Another, inevitably, has been the development of a religious musical practice profoundly affected by those same forces which give secular Gaelic folk music its unique qualities. These two factors acting together resulted in the evolution of a type of psalm singing in which extempore melodic variation of certain old psalm tunes was carried to extremes. The principle is akin to that of *piobaireachd*, each note becoming the focus of a prolonged melismatic decoration, to such an extent that even a listener with a trained ear, and knowing the basic tune, may have difficulty in following. To an outsider hearing this music for the first time the effect may be both puzzling and extremely painful. But some familiarity with the actual sound of the singing, and with the undeviating basic principles lying behind it, brings a fascination and interest that are difficult to describe to anybody who has never heard it. This music of the church, a true folk art, is on the way to extinction. The B.B.C. has made some effort to extend its life by including examples, usually recorded, in broadcast Gaelic services; and it may be heard from within or without the buildings of the various denominations in predominantly Protestant islands such as Harris and Lewis. If the experience should prove unnerving to one hearing this music for the first time, my advice is to persevere, for it is the last remnant of a fascinating and wholly genuine folk art. The School of Scottish Studies has built up a large collection of recordings, so that sooner or later, I hope, we shall have a complete and detailed study of the subject.

Scottish 'Classical' Music

Scotland had not, until near the present century, made any significant *continuing* contribution to music as a conscious and deliberate art; an impartial study of the evidence in printed and MS. sources and in the accounts and memoirs of interested parties, can, alas, raise only very limited pride, enthusiasm or even interest in the heart of a native Scot. A few Renaissance composers (of whom all but one possessed very limited gifts), and a small handful — including a couple of talented aristocratic amateurs — in the eighteenth century do not make an impressive showing. If Scottish music had not taken a new direction about a hundred years ago, this chapter would scarcely have been worth writing.

No doubt there is a tangle of social, historical and geographical reasons why this should have been so; no doubt, too, that Scotland's population was not very large before the Industrial Revolution. Nevertheless, a given total of human beings must contain a certain number with musical gifts which will show themselves *if the circumstances are propitious*. Scotland's record in the literary and visual arts is notable by any standard, and one must conclude that opportunities for talent and even genius to come to fruition have been more favourable than in the case of music.

Not until the nineteenth century was past midway did a climate conducive to the sustained development of musical talent begin to appear. Because that climate has continued fair a context has gradually been formed in which latent musical ability can show itself, be properly nurtured, and be tested against standards other than those of the parish pump.

For this reason, quite a large part of what follows is concerned more with people who helped to create the conditions than with composers, and the latter's part in developing the context may seem to loom quite as large as their actual compositions. I believe that this really is the case and that as a result conditions have evolved, and are still evolving, which allow Scottish musical talent to flourish. He would be a bold man who claimed that Scotland had yet thrown up any twentieth-century musical geniuses; but her chance of doing so has never been so favourable.

The fullest treatment of the subject to date is Dr Henry Farmer's *History of Music in Scotland*, published in 1947. It is a loving, enthusiastic, scrupulously researched and documented book, but it gives the impression of a succession of creative and executant professional and amateur Scottish musicians, backed at times by a strong body of foreign residents, engaged in the thankless task of making bricks with a very minimum of straw. Kenneth Elliott, too, in his contribution to the short history published in 1973 by the B.B.C., finds himself compelled to concentrate on a very small number of known composers, and to indulge in a good deal of optimistic speculation about anonymous ones whose claim even to be Scottish is sometimes flimsy. David Johnson, writing in 1972 about eighteenth-century Scottish music, exaggerates the merits of his key figures *faute de mieux*; earlier, I mentioned big fishes in little ponds and that, I am afraid, is true of almost all Scottish composers before the present century.

Nothing is known of any secular Scottish music before the sixteenth century except for ballad and folk song. The rather meagre sources do, however, reveal that a certain amount of vocal and instrumental music existed at that time; most of it is pleasant and rather superficial, of the kind then enjoyed by the upper clases all over Europe. Little of it can with certainty be attributed to any known composer: of the forty-two examples from the sixteenth and early seventeenth centuries printed by Elliott in *Music of Scotland*; the composers of only four are named with certainty, and of four others conjecturally. French influence is strong, hardly surprisingly in view of the political and military 'auld alliance' between Scotland and France; indeed it is almost certain that some of the songs are Scottish adaptations of French compositions. Some of these works are undeniably fresh, gay and enjoyable, but only the most ardent patriot would claim that they represent a significant contribution to the mainstream of European music. This may be less true of the keyboard works of William Kinloch, whose few surviving compositions are superior in technique and invention to many a piece in the *Fitzwilliam Virginal Book*.

As for the seventeenth century, not even Henry Farmer, with his extraordinary capacity for digging up new evidence of musical activity and talent, could find much good to say. The union of the crowns of Scotland and England in 1603 meant that the Court removed from Edinburgh to London, and with it went any stimulus to composers to provide the sort of music that aristocratic patronage might have called for. As the century progressed, Presbyterian fanaticism sought to stamp out music-making of every kind (except for the twelve psalm tunes). Singing and piping, even at weddings and other social occasions, became a furtive gesture of defiance, liable to fines and other punishments at the behest of the Holy Willies. To us, in a society whose habits have swung almost as far in the other direction, it seems almost unbelievable that a Kirk Session had the power to ordain that 'no person shall suffer any pipes to play at their houses or yards in time coming under pain of 40s. each person'. We know it was common practice to take the risk involved in defying the kill-joys, but the climate ruled out any idea of serious composition. Far into the nineteenth century the General Assembly of the Church of Scotland, and the individual Kirk Sessions (not to mention innumerable breakaway factions) fulminated against music as a passport to Hell. I have actually seen a crude painting depicting the devil seated on a fiery throne, encouraging his toasting-fork-wielding minions to torture crowds of the damned swimming in a pool of burning sulphur, and those damned were drunkards, gamblers, whores and musicians. But the efforts of the 'unco guid' became little by little less effective, and finished up as a squabble about the morals of those who allowed the organ during worship.

The seventeenth century, then, which saw such spectacular musical developments in other parts of Europe, can be written off so far as Scotland is concerned.

Though the eighteenth century did not see the renaissance of genuine Scottish music (that was still a long way off), it at least saw the gradual emergence of a public opinion which tolerated, and as time went on encouraged, music as a desirable part of civilised life. Certain scholars have gone too far in acclaiming this revolution in attitudes to music. David Johnson opines that the years 1760-80 saw a renaissance but, as he admits, it was a brief one—the baby, like Queen Anne's children, scarce had time to look around before its inherent weakness carried it off to a premature grave.

I have already mentioned Allan Ramsay's efforts, in 1724, to bring 'respectability' to Scottish folk song with his *Tea-table Miscellany*. Despite all its faults and weaknesses, Ramsay's work acted as a catalyst for all kinds of reactions from which emerged Scottish National Music—in song, in fiddling, in piping and, not least, in notice being taken of events in the world of music furth of Scotland.

Two Scottish aristocrats who studied composition with famous masters abroad gave an air of respectability to the art. Near the beginning of the century Sir John Clerk, a pupil of Corelli in Italy, left us a small collection of charming compositions. They were original in the sense that they were all his own work, but are essentially imitative of his master's style. Unfortunately, Clerk regarded his musical interests as a mere pastime, and on entering a career in the public service, he abandoned composition altogether.

Later in the century Thomas Erskine, 6th Earl of Kellie, studied in Mannheim under Johann Stamitz. Erskine was an eccentric aristocrat, and his semi-professional activities in composing and publishing music certainly made him appear no less so in the eyes of his peers. His symphonies and chamber music show that, as a composer, he was neither better nor worse than scores of minor European composers engaged in developing the *galant* style of the time; there is very little sign of a personal idiom, and certainly no particularly Scottish quality. Nevertheless, Kellie is not to be dismissed lightly, for he introduced to Edinburgh the new kind of music being developed by the Mannheim composers, and thus played an early part in liberating Scottish music from the shackles of its baleful past.

Subscription concerts were first given in Edinburgh about the beginning of the century and later in other Scottish cities. They were dominated by Italian musicians, and the music was of the kind which they customarily performed in London and elsewhere—the standard instrumental and vocal repertoire of their day. Moving from baroque to classical as the century progressed, they seldom showed any tendency to promote Scottish music, despite the occasional sonata or concerto into which a European composer such as J. C. Bach might introduce a Scottish air as theme for a rondo or set of variations. Compositions by the Earl of Kellie appeared frequently in his lifetime at concerts in Edinburgh, but programmes contained little else of native origin.

After 1780, the conditions in which Scottish successors to Kellie might have flourished began to deteriorate. Interest in semi-public concerts of classical music dwindled, for social reasons too complicated to discuss here. Hopes for the emergence of a new, truly native music were deferred for the best part of another century. Apart from certain aspects of national music shown in works like *The Scots Musical Museum*, Scotland had to be content with a very second-rate, even if fairly numerous, band of native musicians. Dr Farmer gives details of many of them, and makes out the best possible case for regarding them as more than hacks who were able to make a living out of music because there was nobody any better; but his enthusiasm and persuasive pen leave one unconvinced. Scotland still awaited the figure who was to lead its native classical music away from the incompetence

D

and lack of imagination which characterised the period from about 1780 to the mid-nineteenth century—Alexander Mackenzie.

Surveying the history of Scottish music over more than a century, certain facts can be stated with certainty: composers of real talent and vision, equipped by natural gift and good training, emerged in increasing numbers; so did singers, instrumental virtuosi and conductors, some of whom achieved international reputations; proper facilities for the training of professional musicians were established and developed to a very high degree; and public performances of music of every kind, not least opera, increased and improved in quality to an unbelievable extent, when one considers the incompetence of the first half of the nineteenth century. The lively musical scene of the 1970s, with its splendid National Opera, several professional orchestras, its teaching facilities in an Academy of Music and Drama and music departments in all four ancient universities, and with its score or more of gifted composers, is no sudden phenomenon, but the result of a steady growth which began with Mackenzie. Even when posterity has done its usual winnowing, these facts will remain; it is not a matter of Scotland suddenly generating a crowd of creative geniuses, but there is for the first time a situation conducive to the proliferation of high-quality work, in which it is possible for Scotland to give birth to an immortal.

Credit for the restoration should not go to Alexander Mackenzie, but to his father, one of a line of humble enough professional musicians in Edinburgh. Mackenzie senior not only recognised his son's talent, but fostered it in his earliest years and, when the boy was only eleven, sent him to Germany for five years' instruction in musical theory and practice, since adequate training facilities were not available at home. It was not so much young Mackenzie's actual studies which were important for the future, as that, at an impressionable age, he was brought into contact with the mainstream of European music. The young man continued his studies in London, where he developed his gifts as a composer and his ability to earn a living as a practical musician. With Parry and Stanford he inaugurated the renaissance in Britain and later, as Principal of the Royal Academy of Music, he exercised a strong influence on the reorganisation of musical education.

Early in his career, Mackenzie laid the ground for an important development which was effectively to widen the Scottish musical horizon, though he did not realise it. He founded a string quartet and invited a young Düsseldorf musician, Friedrich Niecks, to join as viola player. Niecks was a highly trained musician, from a family of musicians, and whereas Mackenzie soon took himself off to greener pastures, fortunately for Scottish music Niecks settled in Dumfries. In 1890 he was appointed to the Reid Chair of Music in the University of Edinburgh, to be succeeded a quarter of a century later by Donald Francis Tovey. The mere presence in Edinburgh of so broad-minded a scholar and musician as Niecks was of immense importance to the well-being of the slowly developing 'context', a fact that has not been sufficiently recognised. It was he who saw that the Faculty of Music in Edinburgh University was properly established, which led to the granting of degrees in Music. The previous appalling, and at times farcical, history of the Reid Chair can be read in Dr Farmer's *History of Music in Scotland*.

Posterity has dealt rather harshly with Mackenzie (as indeed it has with Parry), and not much of his large output of original music is heard nowadays. He lived and worked during a period when nationalist ideas were being translated in terms of music, and some of his compositions have a pronounced, if rather self-conscious, Scottish flavour. He was not a good judge of words, and some of his compositions are unperformable on account of their disastrously poor libretti.

Mackenzie's activities cleared the way for the next generation, and a gifted lot they were. They showed, in their grasp of the sophisticated post-Wagnerian techniques of their time, that skill and craftsmanship were as likely to be found among Scotsmen as anywhere else. Most of them were romantic in outlook and expression, and much influenced by Wagner and Brahms. They tried to develop a 'Scottishness' in their work, and because of it are referred to as the 'nationalist' group. But they were not a group at all, rather a number of individuals, among whom Learmont Drysdale, Hamish MacCunn, W. B. Moonie, David Stephen, William Wallace and John B. McEwen are best remembered. Their contribution to the growing body of Scottish compositions was large, and far more important than most young sophisticates of today are willing to admit. This is particularly true of MacCunn and McEwen; the latter's music reflects, on the whole, the harsher side of Scottish life and character in the same way as Sibelius's music reflects Finland. Of all his generation, McEwen is the one most likely to be resurrected at some future date.

Wallace and McEwen were deeply involved in training young musicians, as was Mackenzie; indeed McEwen, like Mackenzie, ended his career as a knight and as Principal of the Royal Academy of Music in London. McEwen bequeathed the residue of his estate to the University of Glasgow to encourage the performance and composition of chamber music by Scottish musicians. The bequest allows for triennial series of concerts of Scottish works, and for the commissioning of new ones annually.

Few of Scotland's leading musicians of the renaissance remained at home—almost all had to seek a wider field in which to make a living from their talent. Public response to the burgeoning of the seeds sown by Mackenzie was slow; old habits die hard, and the Scots are particularly prone to disparage home-bred talent. There is a much-quoted Scottish version of the 'prophet without honour' tag which sums up the matter—"Him a famous musician—dinna be daft, I kent his faither!" These words in a sense encapsulate the Scottish character, and suggest that complex combination of the hair shirt, self-depreciation and boastfulness which has often been an obstacle to the relaxed development of natural gifts and characteristics.

The next group of Scottish composers, if for convenience a number of individualists may again be brought together, covers the period from the 1920s to post-World War Two. Two of them are still living, of whom one has not been very active as a composer since the 60s. The principal figures, in order of birth, are Francis George Scott, Ian Whyte, Erik Chisholm, Robin Orr and Cedric Thorpe Davie. Before having a brief glance at the work of each it must be said that these composers played a considerable part in changing public attitudes to serious music in general, and to Scottish serious music in particular. In their time, a large number of Scots ceased to believe that any indigenous Scottish music must by definition be contemptible and started, very gradually, to relate the native product to the international world of music. This education of an appreciative public was very slow, and the process of enlarging the audience went on in the teeth of much prejudice, ignorance and indifference.

The B.B.C. in Scotland—particularly during the musical directorship of a dedicated administrator named Herbert Wiseman—was responsible to a great extent for the change. It was at the start of Wiseman's reign that Ian Whyte took over the permanent conductorship of the B.B.C. Scottish Symphony Orchestra. By giving many and repeated performances of Scottish compositions, Whyte showed the public that real talent was among them, and encouraged the composers themselves with the prospect of actually hearing their large-scale works. Earlier in his career, Wiseman had been very influential in a revolution which took place in the musical education of schoolchildren. Professional study of the higher branches of music was profoundly affected by the occupation of the key positions of Professor of Music at the Universities of Edinburgh and Glasgow for many years by two great English musicians, D. F. Tovey and W. G. Whittaker. They brought to Scottish music an understanding of historical perspective and of the international scene which had never been known before. Whittaker encountered a great deal of parochially motivated opposition to his broad-minded planning, and was forced to waste much time and energy in fighting to impose and maintain standards of integrity which were incomprehensible to his critics. His powerful influence, however, can be felt to this day. Gradually, these and many lesser devoted figures created a context in which latent talent could appear and develop.

It was in this improving climate that Scott, Whyte, Chisholm, Orr and Davie were able to remain in, or to return to, their native country for a part or the whole of their careers, and to earn a living among their own countrymen — a radical difference from the group which preceded them. It is true that in middle age Chisholm left home to become Professor of Music in the University of Cape Town, but only after his vitality and enthusiasm had made a lasting mark upon the Scottish musical scene, particularly in Glasgow. Scott, as lecturer in music in Glasgow's principal college for the training of schoolteachers, played a vital part in the expansion of musical education; Whyte's work as conductor and propagator has already been mentioned; Orr, the least prolific of the group, spent the first part of his musical life as an organist and teacher in the University of Cambridge. He later became Professor of Music at the University of Glasgow, during which period much of his most important music was composed, and he ultimately returned to Cambridge as Professor of Music in that university; Davie founded and developed a new music department in the University of St Andrews, where he eventually became Professor.

Thus, all five creative musicians, in company with a great number of devoted workers less in the public eye, played important parts in bringing Scotland into the big world of music. Ironically it may prove that in doing so these composers, all of whom endeavoured to give their music some distinctively Scottish quality, actually brought about a reaction in their successors, whose aim, it will possibly be found, may be at non-national targets in styles and idioms accepted worldwide, and in competition with composers not only from Europe and America, but from African and Asian countries which have until recently made virtually no impact on the international scene.

Francis George Scott (1880-1958) was primarily a lyricist of fastidious taste, and it is as a songwriter that he is likely to be remembered. He was at his best when joining his subtle and inventive gifts to those of Scottish poets who were his contemporaries and friends, particularly Hugh MacDiarmid. On the whole, his settings of poems by Burns (who intended them to be sung, be it remembered, to melodies of his own choice) are less convincing. Scott has suffered badly from over-praise by amateurs with little understanding of music, and from professionals who should have known better. Little good can come to the reputation of a creative artist of modest pretensions and quite exceptional sensitivity from absurd comparisons with Schubert. Scott's work is unique, it speaks for itself, and it remains by far the highest contribution by a Scotsman to a particular, if restricted, branch of the art of music.

Ian Whyte (1901-60) cast his net much wider that Scott did, and wrote operas, ballets, symphonies, concertos, chamber music and a great deal of occasional music for radio productions. He was intensely self-critical, to the point, it sometimes seemed, of being unsure of himself; he tended to self-examination and to rather hair-shirted doubts of his own sincerity. He had a masterly technical control of the resources of modern music and an ear of phenomenal acuteness.

Erik Chisholm (1904-65), who came of a family little interested in music, encountered much opposition to his ideas, which in 1930 were regarded as *avant-garde*. He was the most prolific of all this group, turning out works (including some dozen operas) at very high speed, sometimes with a cheerful disregard for detail. He made most serious attempts to integrate the spirit of Scottish national music into his writing, and particularly sought inspiration in *piobaireachd,* whose principles, and particularly whose complex melodic convolutions, he sought to bring into the larger world of instrumental composition. In this, and in his earlier music in general, the influence of his hero, the Hungarian Béla Bartók, can be clearly seen.

Robin Orr (b. 1909) probably shows fewer signs of Scottishness in his compositions than do others of the group, possibly because the earlier part of his career was bound up with English university life. So far as public recognition goes, however, it was after he returned to his native country that he came to the fore, particularly with his symphony and with two operas which were staged by Scottish Opera.

Cedric Thorpe Davie (b. 1913), the youngest of the group, learned his trade in London. Among his teachers was Vaughan Williams, whose style profoundly influenced his work, as did Sibelius. His knack of writing effectively at high speed for film, theatre and radio may have drawn him away to some extent from more permanent forms, of which his output is rather scanty compared with Whyte or Chisholm. A good deal of his work was designed for performance by young people or amateurs, with whom he was associated during his long academic life at the University of St Andrews.

It is worth noting that the renaissance brought with it a remarkable upsurge of Scottish executant talent, both individual and collective. In the late nineteenth and early twentieth centuries, certain Scottish-born players and singers such as Frederick Lamond, Mary Garden, Joseph Hyslop and Murray Dickie achieved world standing as performing artists. But their training was elsewhere, and their reputations had nothing to do with their Scottishness; they were, simply, international figures some of whom, by the law of averages, are bound to be born in the northern part of Great Britain. With the improving musical climate, and with the growth of opportunities for teaching at the highest level, there appeared a number of superb teachers in Glasgow, Edinburgh and elsewhere. Among the earliest were the pianists Philip Halstead and Ailie Cullen and the violinist Bessie Spence. Ailie Cullen was one of the finest accompanists and lieder pianists of any country or time. Thereafter fine teachers appeared in growing numbers, whose names cannot all be given here, and from whom it would be invidious to make any selection. Their pupils include several high-ranking opera singers, conductors—Sir Alexander Gibson, for example—and instrumentalists of all kinds. Similarly, the growing enterprise and reputations of the departments of music in Scotland's four ancient universities attracted scholars and research workers to continue what had been so admirably begun by Niecks, Tovey and Whittaker.

Sir Alexander Gibson, backed by splendid production and administrative staffs and by funds from the Scottish Arts Council and private sources, developed the Scottish National Orchestra and Scottish Opera into permanent organisations of international reputation. The spin-off from their success can be seen in the founding of such bodies as the Scottish Chamber Orchestra and the Scottish Baroque Ensemble. Arthur Oldham and John Currie organised professional and amateur choruses which they trained to a pitch of virtuosity and excellence unimagined in the first half of the century when Scottish choirs, excellent in their way, aspired only to polished accounts of madrigals and part songs. Never in his wildest dreams could Mackenzie have envisaged the ceaseless musical activity which was to spring from his teenage years in Germany.

The outstanding work of Frederick Rimmer must be mentioned before I close this survey. An Englishman, but Scottish by adoption, Rimmer spent most of his musical career in Glasgow, eventually succeeding Robin Orr as Professor in Glasgow University. I have referred several times to the development of an environment in which it is possible for musicians, and especially composers, to flourish; Rimmer is an accomplished organist and a considerable composer, but his chief importance to Scottish music is due to the opportunities arising from his official position as head of an influential university department. He was largely responsible for founding and developing the Scottish Music Archive, in which copies and recordings of Scottish works are catalogued, stored, and made available to the public. The Archive is funded by the Scottish Arts Council, the

Scottish universities (particularly Glasgow, where it is housed), and by a number of public and private bodies. Rimmer's persistence and enthusiasm for new thinking in music stimulated the modern generation of Scottish composers (some of whom are his pupils) in several important ways. He was primarily responsible for the installation of a very fine electronic workshop in his department, whose facilities are made available not only to the University's students and researchers, but to other bona fide Scottish composers. He was the motivating force behind the McEwen Memorial concerts in the university, for which new Scottish works are commissioned annually. In collaboration with Sir Alexander Gibson and the Scottish National Orchestra, he was responsible for what has come to be known as Musica Nova, a periodic event in Glasgow at which new works by Scottish and other contemporary composers are played and studied. All this is a splendid and fitting development of the work of pioneers like Wiseman and Whittaker.

Let us look now at the composition of original works of music of the late twentieth century. The difficulty in discussing contemporary matters is that what is true today is likely to be out of date tomorrow. I will attempt to give a sketch of the scene as it is in 1980, but I cannot even speculate on what the picture will look like by 1990. Some names which are bandied about in musical circles will be forgotten in ten years, and those of some other bright young people will have replaced them; this, I hope, will explain and excuse the tentative and superficial nature of these final paragraphs.

At least three leading English composers have chosen to take up residence in Scotland. This does not make them Scotsmen, nor does it necessarily mean that there is or will be anything particularly Scottish about their work. However, it is significant that Kenneth Leighton, William Wordsworth and Peter Maxwell Davies should have *chosen* to live and work in a country which, only a little more than a century ago, was virtually a musical desert. Maxwell Davies has striven to identify himself with his adopted home, and has led the latent musical talent of remote Orkney into a much-discussed role in the *avant-garde* of British music.

Never in Scotland's history has so much native-born musical talent come to the surface. The Scottish Composers' Guild has more than thirty members, many of them born since the war, and all serious in their artistic intentions. It is impossible to keep track of all their work—which covers styles and idioms from the conservative to the experimental —or to make any sort of valid assessment of its ultimate worth. Today's best-known names are probably Martin Dalby, David Dorward, Ian Hamilton, Thea Musgrave and Thomas Wilson. Of these, at least two have international reputations, and this may be because parts of their lives have been spent abroad. Scottish Opera has mounted productions of full-scale operas by Hamilton, Musgrave and Wilson.

More than most of his contemporaries, Thomas Wilson seems anxious to preserve a positive Scottish quality in his work. But there appears to be a tendency—certainly among the younger composers—to draw inspiration from international, rather than from national sources, and to take as models composers like Stockhausen and Xenakis rather than to continue the work of Whyte and Chisholm. If this generation had more opportunities to hear the work of their immediate forebears, things might be different.

There is no more unprofitable pastime than speculation on the judgements of posterity. The desire to have one's work remembered and approved by future generations, natural though it may be, is futile and emotionally wasteful. Scotland is littered with hilltop monuments erected to the memories of ironmasters, generals, professors, parsons and so on—often with funds left by themselves for the purpose—which have become objects of derision rather than of the veneration hoped for by their sponsors. Our newspapers and journals are full of so-called criticism by sit-on-the-wall writers who are damned sure *they* are not going to be laughed at, as we laugh at the *Harmonicon* critic of the 1820s who averred that the 'Hammerklavier' sonata provided evidence that Beethoven had finally gone round the bend. Nobody can say which, if any, of the works of living Scottish composers will be thought of as significant or influential by our great-grandchildren; nor ought the fact to be regarded with regret. Rather, Scots should be proud and joyful that at last their country is taking a positive part in a civilising process in a world much in need of anti-Philistine activity. It is the business of Scottish musicians, whether as composers or performers, scholars, teachers or administrators, to get on with their jobs and see to it that their country never again becomes a musical Sahara.

Select Bibliography

THE following works have a direct bearing on the subjects discussed in the text. Titles are given in chronological order of first publication, but most have appeared in subsequent editions, and several have been reprinted in facsimile in recent years.

1733   William Thomson (ed.), *Orpheus Caledonius*, 2nd edition, 2 vols.

1747   James Oswald, *The Caledonian Pocket Companion*, 12 parts

1787   James Johnson, *The Scots Musical Museum*, 6 vols.

1794   Joseph Ritson, *Scotish Songs*, 2 vols. Important introductory essay

1848   G. F. Graham (ed.), *The Songs of Scotland*, 3 vols. Fully annotated

1853   William Stenhouse, *Illustrations of the Lyric Poetry and Music of Scotland*

1864   Rev. Neil Livingston, *The Scottish Metrical Psalter of 1635*

1894   David Baptie, *Musical Scotland*. A useful dictionary of Scottish musicians up to the end of the nineteenth century

1898   Wm C. Honeyman, *Scottish Violin Makers Past and Present*

1900   John Glen, *Early Scottish Melodies*. An invaluable study, particularly concerned with *The Scots Musical Museum*

1903   James C. Dick, *The Songs of Robert Burns*. The introductory essay has never been superseded

1947   Henry Farmer, *The History of Music in Scotland*. A valuable and detailed study of the whole field

1949   Rev. Miller Patrick, *Four Centuries of Scottish Psalmody*. A full and absorbing account, written with love and a great deal of humour

1959   Bernard H. Bronson, *The Traditional Tunes of the Child Ballads*, 4 vols.

1964   Kenneth Elliott (ed.), *Music of Scotland*, being Vol. XV of the series 'Musica Britannica'

1966 Francis Collinson, *The Traditional and National Music of Scotland*. Very detailed in its account of folk music

1968 Seumas MacNeill, *Piobaireachd*. A very clear short exposition

1969 Cedric Thorpe Davie and George McVicar (eds.), *The Oxford Scottish Song Book*

1972 David Johnson, *Music and Society in Lowland Scotland in the 18th Century*. A brilliant book by a young writer, sometimes wayward in its judgements but fascinating in the clarity of its exposition of a number of aspects

1973 Kenneth Elliott and Frederick Rimmer, *A History of Scottish Music*. A valuable short summary published by the B.B.C.

1979 James Hunter (ed.), *The Fiddle Music of Scotland*

1980 Maurice Lindsay, *Francis George Scott and the Scottish Renaissance*

     Alistair Campsie, *The MacCrimmon Legend*. An outspoken questioning of some of the piping world's most cherished beliefs

Those who wish to pursue the subject of Robert Burns's contribution to Scottish National Music are recommended to consult:

Cuthbert Hadden, *The Life of George Thomson*
James Kinsley (ed.), *The Poems and Songs of Robert Burns*
Donald Low (ed.), *Critical Essays on Robert Burns*
Catarina Ericson-Roos, *The Songs of Robert Burns*